LET'S GO Map Guide
Madrid

Alexa M. Gutheil
Editor

Nina Mitchell
Researcher-Writer

St. Martin's Press ≋ New York

A NOTE TO OUR READERS

The information for this book is gathered by Let's Go researchers during the summer months. Each listing is derived from the assigned researcher's opinion based upon his or her visit at a particular time. The opinions are expressed in a candid and forthright manner. Other travelers might disagree. Those traveling at a different time may have different experiences since prices, dates, hours, and conditions are always subject to change. You are urged to check beforehand to avoid inconvenience and surprises. Travel always involves a certain degree of risk, especially in low-cost areas. When traveling, especially on a budget, you should always take particular care to ensure your safety.

HELPING LET'S GO

If you want to share your discoveries, suggestions, or corrections, please drop us a line. All suggestions are passed along to our researcher-writers. **Address mail to:**

> **Let's Go Map Guide: Madrid**
> **67 Mount Auburn Street**
> **Cambridge, MA 02138**
> **USA**

Visit Let's Go at **http://www.letsgo.com,** or send e-mail to:

> **fanmail@letsgo.com**

Contents

How to Use This Map Guide

Let's Go Map Guide: Madrid is made up of two parts: a detailed fold-out map and a short pamphlet of information on getting around, getting by, and getting out in Madrid. To integrate the two parts, we have included a detailed street index at the end of the guide. Using the index, addresses and street names given in the listings can be placed in the context of the city at large. In addition, certain important sights are marked by numbered red squares on the maps. The numbers correspond to numbers on the List of Sights found on the last page of the guide. The List of Sights features page numbers for many of the sights, to help you quickly find related write-ups and reviews. In the text, the number of any sight marked on the map follows the name or phone number of the sight. Thus, you can easily find the location of a sight you've read about.

Useful Phone Numbers

Emergency: tel. 092 (national police) or 091 (local).
Accommodations Services: Viajes Brújula (tel. 559 97 04). I
the airport (tel. 305 86 56).
Airport: Aeropuerto de Barajas (24-hr. tel. 305 83 43). **Iber**
(tel. 587 81 56). **American Airlines** (597 20 68). **TWA** (310 60). **British Airways** (tel. 431 75 75).
American Express: (tel. 322 55 00). Lost checks (24-hr. tel 900 44 26). Other problems (24-hr. tel. 900 94 14 13).
Automobile Assistance: RACE (tel. 593 33 33 or 900 11 22).
Automobile Rental: Autos Bravo (tel. 474 80 75). **Autos Vi** ducto (tel. 548 48 48). **Auto Compartido** (tel. 522 77 72).
Budget Travel Organizations: Viajes Tive (tel. 543 02 08
Dirección General de la Joventud (tel. 580 42 16). **Viaje**
Lanzani (tel. 541 47 32). **Viva** (tel. 531 10 00).
Buses: Bus-Aeropuerto (tel. 431 61 92). **Estación Sur d**
Autobuses (tel. 468 42 00). **Estación Auto Res** (tel. 551 72 00
Estación La Sepulvedana (tel. 530 48 00).
Directory Assistance: Info tel. 010 or 003.
Embassies:
U.S. (tel. 577 40 00).
Australia (tel. 579 04 28).
U.K. (tel. 319 02 00).
Canada (tel. 431 43 00).
Ireland (tel. 576 35 00).
New Zealand (tel. 523 02 26).
Fire Department: tel. 080.
Help and Crisis Lines:
AIDS Information and Hotline (tel. 445 23 28).
Alcoholics Anonymous (tel. 309 19 47).
Disabled Access Information (tel. 413 74 41).
Drug Abuse Hotline (tel. 900 16 15 15).
English Language Helpline (tel. 559 13 93).
Gay and Lesbian Helpline (tel. 522 45 17).
Poision Control (tel. 562 04 00).
Rape Hotline (tel. 574 01 10).
Women's Issues (tel. 900 19 10 10).
Hospital: Anglo-American Medical Unit: tel. 435 18 2
Emergency Health Clinic: (tel. 358 08 51).
Parks and Recreation: Dirección General de Deportes (ge eral sporting info; tel. 409 49 04). **Casa de Campo** (swimmin tel. 463 00 50). **Ciclos Muñoz** (biking; tel. 475 02 19).
Pharmacy: Late-night (info tel. 098).
Public Transportation Authority: Metro information (te 552 50 09). **Bus information** (tel. 401 99 00). **Taxis** (tel. 445 9 08).
Police (non-emergency): tel. 521 12 36.
Post Office: tel. 536 01 10.
Red Cross: tel. 429 19 60.
Sporting Arenas: Estadio Santiago Bernebéu (fútbol, Re Madrid; tel. 457 11 12). **Estadio Vicente Calderón** (fútbo Atlético de Madrid; tel. 366 47 07). **Hipódromo de Madri** (horse racing; tel. 357 16 82). **Plaza de Ventas** (bullfights; tel. 22 00).
Tourist Offices: Municipal (tel. 366 54 77). **Regional/Provir cial** (tel. 902 10 00). **In the airport** (tel. 305 86 56).
Trains: RENFE (tel. 328 90 20). **Chamartín** (24-hr. tel. 323 2 21). **Atocha** (tel. 527 31 60).
Transportation Police: tel. 521 09 11.
Weather: tel. 094.

Madrid

Although it witnessed the coronation of Fernando and Isabel, Madrid was of no great importance until Habsburg King Felipe II moved the Spanish court here permanently in 1561—an unlikely choice for a capital considering the city's distance from vital ports and rivers. Nonetheless, the city became a seat of wealth, culture, and imperial glory, overseeing Spain's 16th- and 17th-century Golden Age of literature (Lope de Vega, Cervantes), art (Velázquez, El Greco), and architecture. Today's Madrid owes much of its neoclassical flair, from the Palacio Real in the west to the Museo del Prado in the east, to Bourbon King Felipe V's 18th-century urban renewal. Wide, leafy boulevards and a general absence of skyscrapers preclude the hyper-urban feel of comparably sized cities. Yet Madrid is anything but a museum piece. The city nourishes an avant-garde social and political scene made famous by Spain's rich crop of contemporary authors and artists. Infinitely energized *madrileños* mingle in cafés and *terrazas* by day, then crowd bars and discos by night and on into the morning. Bright lights and a perpetual stream of automobile and pedestrian traffic blur the distinction between 4pm and 4am. The capital of contemporary Spanish political and cultural life, surpassing Barcelona as the country's manufacturing and financial center, Madrid exudes a remarkable energy and vitality which make it a fitting symbol of Spain's newfound status as a leading European nation.

PRACTICAL INFORMATION

Tourist Offices: Those planning trips outside the Communidad de Madrid can visit region-specific offices within Madrid; ask the tourist offices below for addresses. **Municipal:** Pl. Mayor, 3 (tel. 366 54 77 or 588 16 36; fax 366 54 77). M: Sol. On the Plaza Mayor. Has city and transport maps, a guide to accommodations, as well as *En Madrid,* a monthly activities guide. Open Mon.-Fri. 10am-8pm, Sat. 10am-2pm. Other offices at **Estación Chamartín** (tel. 315 99 76) and the **airport** (tel. 305 86 56), in the international arrivals area (both open Mon.-Fri. 8am-8pm, Sat. 9am-1pm).

Tours: Read the fine print before paying an arm and a leg for a walk around the block. The following are geared towards tourists, given in English. **Pullmantur,** Pl. Oriente, 8 (tel. 541 18 05, 06, or 07). M: Ópera. Tours of Madrid average around 4000ptas. Also excursions to outlying areas. Prices include transportation and admission to museums and monuments. **Trapsatur,** San Bernardo, 23 (tel. 542 66 66). M: Santo Domingo.

General Info Line: tel. 010. Run by the Ayuntamiento (City Hall), they'll tell you anything about Madrid, from the nearest police station's address to zoo hours. **Info:** tel. 003. No English spoken.

Budget Travel: Viajes TIVE: C. Fernando el Católico, 88 (tel. 543 02 08 or 543 74 12; fax 544 00 62). M: Moncloa. No commissions. Discount airfares and ticket sales. BIJ train tickets. ISIC 700ptas. HI cards 1800ptas. Excursions and language classes. Message board with rides, cheap tickets, and apartment notices. Open Mon.-Fri. 9am-2pm, Sat. 9am-noon. Arrive early. English spoken.

Currency Exchange: American Express has competitive rates for traveler's checks. **Banco Central Hispano** also has no commission and good rates for American Express traveler's checks. Banks (1-2% commission, 500ptas min. charge), El Corte Inglés, and even four- and five-star hotels offer exchange services at varying rates. Those places open on weekends and as late as 2am, such as Exact Change, Cambios-Uno, and Chequepoint, are not a good deal for cashing traveler's checks: they have no commission and small (250-300ptas) minimum charges, but poor rates. On the other hand, for small-denomination bills (e.g., US$20 or US$50) they may be the best option. Many are at Sol and on the Gran Vía. **ATMs** are plenti-

ful; the **Servi Red, Servi Caixa,** and **Telebanco** machine
accept bank cards with one or more of the Cirrus, PLUS, an
NYCE logos. Be forewarned: use only the first four digits of you
PIN code. Spanish machines operate only with numbers, not le
ters—if your PIN code is your cat's name, be sure you know i
numerical translation.

American Express: Pl. Cortes, 2 (tel. 322 55 00). M: Sevill
"Agencia de Viajes" is written on the windows. **Currenc
exchange** (1% cash and 2% traveler's check commission; n
commission on AmEx traveler's checks; no min. charge). They
hold mail for 30 days and send and receive wired money. In a
emergency, AmEx cashes personal checks up to US$1000 fc
cardholders. Express Cash machine. To report or cancel lost tra
eler's checks, call 24-hr. toll-free (900) 99 44 26. To report othe
problems, call (900) 94 14 13. Open Mon.-Fri. 9am-5:30pm, Sa
9am-noon.

El Corte Inglés: C. Preciados, 3 (tel. 532 18 00). M: Sol. C. Goy
76 (tel. 577 71 71). M: Goya. C. Princesa, 42 (tel. 542 48 00). M
Argüelles. C. Raimundo Fernández Villaverde, 79 (tel. 556 23 00
M: Nuevos Ministerios. Giant chain of department stores. **Cu
rency exchange:** Commission included in their mediocre rate
Good **map,** haircutting, *cafetería* and restaurant, **supermar
ket, telephones,** tapes and CDs, books in English, electronic
Open Mon.-Sat. 10am-9pm, Sun. 10am-2pm.

Telephones: Telefónica, Gran Vía, 30, at C. Valverde. M: Gra
Vía. Direct-dial lines to the U.S. at exorbitant rates. Open dai
9:30am-11:30pm. Calls over 500ptas can be charged to a cred
card. Long-distance calls may also be placed at Po. Recoletos, 4
off Pl. Colón (both open Mon.-Fri. 8am-midnight, Sat.-Sun. an
holidays 8am-10pm). **Tarjetas telefónicas** (telephone cards
sold at Telefónica or **tabacos** shops in 1000ptas and 2000p
denominations, save you from change-guzzling public phones.

Luggage Storage: Estaciones de Chamartín and Atoch
Lockers at the *consigna* and *largo recorrido* areas. Small ba
300ptas per day, medium 400ptas, large 600ptas. Open 6:30ar
12:30am. **Estación Sur de Autobus:** Bags checked (800ptas

Laundromats: All laundromats have drying services—price va
ies depending on size of load or drying time. **Lavanderí
Donoso Cortés,** C. Donoso Cortés, 17 (tel. 446 96 90). M: Qu
vedo. From the station, walk down C. Bravo Murillo to C. Donos
Cortés. Self-service: wash 600ptas, detergent 70ptas (open Mor
Fri. 9am-7pm, Sat. 8:30am-1pm).

Taxes and Tipping: As an EU country, Spain tags a 7% Valu
Added Tax on most goods; as a VAT, the tax is usually included i
the quoted price. The rate is less on such items as food, wate
prescription drugs, and hotel stays. Visitors in Spain for less tha
180 days can get a VAT refund at the airport; make sure you ge
the forms at the time of purchase. Most restaurants add in a se
vice charge to bills, but it is customary to round to the next hig
est unit of currency as an additional tip; 5-10% is normal. Porte
and taxi drivers are often tipped as well. In general, Spaniards c
not expect large tips.

Women's Services: Librería de Mujeres, C. San Cristóba
17 (tel. 521 70 43), near Pl. Mayor. M: Sol. Books and gifts; main
for Spanish speakers (open Mon.-Fri. 10am-2pm and 5-8pm, Sa
10am-2pm). **Women's Info/Issues,** tel. 900 19 10 10.

**Gay and Lesbian Services: The Colectivo de Gais y Le
bianas de Madrid (COGAM),** C. Espiritus Santo, 37 (tel./fa
522 45 17) directly across from the Ministry of Justice. M: Nov
ciado. Provides a wide range of services and activities of intere
to gays, lesbians, bisexuals, transsexuals, and others (receptic
open Mon.-Fri. 5-9pm). Free counseling Mon.-Thurs. 7-9pm
GAI-INFORM, a gay info line (tel. 523 00 70; Mon.-Fri. 5-9pm
provides info in Spanish about gay associations and issues. Th
same number has info on Brujulai, COGAM's weekend excursi

group. **Colectivo de Feministas Lesbianas de Madrid (CFLM),** tel. 319 36 89.

Help Lines: AIDS Info Hotline (tel. 445 23 28). **Detox** (tel. 900 16 15 15). No English. **Alcohólicos Anónimos,** C. Juan Bravo, 40, 2nd fl. (tel. 309 19 47 in English; crisis line in Spanish 532 30 30). M: Núñez de Balboa. **English-Language Helpline** (tel. 559 13 93), for confidential help from trained volunteers 7-11pm.

Crisis Lines: Poison Control (tel. 562 04 00). **Rape Hotline** (tel. 574 01 10). No English spoken.

Late-Night Pharmacy: (Info tel. 098). Check *Farmacias de Guardia* listings in local papers to find pharmacies open after 8pm. Lists of the nearest on-duty pharmacy are also posted in all pharmacy windows. Contraceptive products are sold over the counter in most Spanish pharmacies.

Hospitals: Most are in the north and east ends of the city. Prompt appointments are hard to obtain (emergency rooms are the best option for immediate attention), but public hospitals here treat patients whether or not they pay in advance. If your Spanish is poor, try the **Anglo-American Medical Unit,** Conde de Aranda, 1, 1st fl. (tel. 435 18 23), to the left. M: Retiro. Doctors, dentists, optometrists. Assistance available at all hours. *Not* an emergency clinic. Embassies and consulates keep lists of English-speaking doctors in private practice. **Hospital Clínico San Carlos,** Pl. Cristo Rey (tel. 330 30 00). M: Moncloa.

Emergency Clinics: Ciudad Sanitaria La Paz, Po. Castellana, 261 (tel. 358 08 51). M: Begoña. **Equipo Quirúrgico Municipal No. 1,** C. Montesa, 22 (tel. 401 80 50). M: Manuel Becerra. **Hospital Ramón y Cajal,** Ctra. de Colmenar Viejo, km. 9100 (tel. 729 00 00). Municipal bus #135 from Pl. Castilla.

Police:. C. Luna, 29 (tel. 521 12 36). M: Callao. From Gran Vía walk down C. Arenal. To report crimes in the Metro, go to the office in the Sol station (tel. 521 09 11). Open 8am-11pm. **Guardia Civil** (tel. 062 or 533 11 00). **Protección Civil** (tel. 537 17 00).

Emergency: call 091 (national police) or 092 (local).

Post Office: Palacio de Comunicaciones, Pl. Cibeles (tel. 396 24 43). M: Banco de España. An enormous, ornate palace on the far side of the plaza from the Metro. Info (door E) open Mon.-Fri. 8am-10pm, or call the useful info line (tel. 537 64 94). Open for stamp purchase and certified mail (main door) Mon.-Fri. 8am-10pm, Sat. 8:30am-8:30pm, Sun. 9:30am-1:30pm; telex and **fax** service open Mon.-Fri. 8am-midnight, Sat.-Sun. 8am-10pm. Windows may change. English and French spoken at info desk. **Postal Code:** 28070. **Telephone Code:** (9)1.

ORIENTATION

The "Kilometro 0" marker on the sidewalk in front of the police station signals the city's epicenter at **Puerta del Sol,** an intersection of eight major streets. Sol is *the* transportation hub of the city: below ground, three Metro lines (blue #1, red #2, yellow #3) converge.. Pta. del Sol itself is packed with restaurants, *cafeterías,* shops, tourists, banks, *hostales,* and services of all kinds.

Madrid is divided into fairly distinct neighborhoods. **Old Madrid,** the nucleus of neighborhoods clustered around Sol, is bordered by the **Palacio Real** to the west, the **Gran Vía** to the north, the **Museo del Prado** to the east, and fades away in the south around **Atocha** (the older train station). Within this nucleus, to the west of Sol, lie the two royal Madrids: red brick Madrid de los Austrias around **Plaza de la Villa** and **Plaza Mayor,** and granite Madrid de los Borbones around **Ópera.** Both neighborhoods are relatively quiet, given over to churches, convents, and historical houses, but *hostales* coexist with the monuments.

Continuing in a clockwise direction, the segment north of Sol is a shopper's paradise—a web of pedestrian-only streets lead past the

Corte Inglés to the Gran Vía (bright lights and big movie theaters). East from Sol, the majestic **Calle de Alcalá** leads out of old Madrid towards broader avenues, eventually passing by the **Parque del Retiro.** South of Alcalá, and between Sol and the Museo del Prado, the old literary district of Madrid is crowded with some of the best value *hostales* in the city as well as some of the best bars and cafés centered on **Plaza Santa Ana.**

Fewer tourists venture directly south of Sol into the area around **La Latina** and **Tirso de Molina** Metro stops; this is a poorer and less flashy part of Old Madrid. **El Rastro,** a gargantuan ancient flea market, is staged here every Sunday morning. Farther south lies **Lavapiés,** a working-class neighborhood that allows for a less touristy sense of the city.

The newer parts of interest lie mainly to the east and north of the old city. To the northwest, the Gran Vía runs up to **Plaza de España,** its tall Torre de Madrid the pride of fifties Spain. From the Plaza, the Gran Vía turns into **Calle Princesa,** a bustling middle class shopping avenue leading to **Moncloa** and **Argüelles,** two increasingly upscale student neighborhoods near the **Ciudad Universitaria.** East of Argüelles, and connected to the Gran Vía by **Calle de Fuencarral** are the two club and bar-hopping districts of **Malasaña** and **Bilbao. Chueca,** basically Bilbao in black and chains, is the next neighborhood to the east. Chueca is bordered by the great north-south backbone of the **Paseo de la Castellana-Paseo de Recoletos-Paseo del Prado** which runs from Atocha in the south to **Plaza Castilla** in the north, passing the Prado, the fountains at **Cibeles** and **Colón,** and the elaborate skyscrapers beyond Colón. East of the Po. de la Castellana and just behind the Museo del Prado, the lush Parque del Retiro functions as a front yard for the posh shopping and residential streets of the **Barrio de Salamanca.**

Madrid is extremely safe compared to other major European cities, but the Puerta del Sol, Plaza 2 de Mayo in Malasaña, Plaza de Chueca, and Plaza de España are particularly intimidating late at night. As a general rule, avoid the parks and quiet residential areas after dark. Watch out for thieves and pickpockets in the Metro and on crowded city streets, and be wary of opportunists who target tourists with their clever scams. The preeminence of the con artist, particularly around Madrid's *centro,* is a tradition which dates far back in Madrid's cultural history.

ARRIVALS AND DEPARTURES

By Plane

All flights land at the **Aeropuerto Internacional de Barajas,** in the town of Barajas, a half hour by car northeast of Madrid. The simplest and cheapest way to get to town is the **Bus-Aeropuerto** (look for EMT signs just outside the doors), which leaves every 15 minutes between 5am and midnight (360ptas).

The Bus-Aeropuerto stops underground beneath the **Plaza de Colón.** Exit from the side of the park with the waterfall and you'll be on Paseo de Recoletos. The Colón Metro station (brown line, #4) is across the street. To get to Puerta del Sol, switch at M: Bilbao to line #1, and ride three stops to M: Sol. By foot, walk left down Po. de Recoletos to the next plaza, Pl. de la Cibeles, turn right down C. de Alcalá, and bear left at the next fork (still Alcalá, 20min.).

A fleet of taxis swarms at the airport. The ride to Pta. del Sol costs 2000-2500ptas, depending on traffic and the number of bags. Some drivers claim not to know the address given to them, or try to take the unwitting traveler to an expensive conspiring hotel. Don't be duped—insist firmly on being taken to your destination or a nearby landmark. Fares from the airport to downtown Madrid should be no more than 3000ptas.

In the airport, a branch of the regional tourist office (tel. 305 86 56) in the international arrivals area has maps and other basics open Mon.-Fri. 8am-8pm, Sat. 9am-1pm). In the airport and at the Bus-Aeropuerto stop in Pl. Colón, branches of the Brújula accommodations service can find visitors places to stay immediately.

Iberia: C. Goya, 29 (tel. 587 81 56). M: Serrano. Open Mon.-Fri. 9:30am-2pm and 4-7pm. For reservations, call 329 43 53 (24hr.).
American Airlines: C. Pedro Texeira, 8 (tel. 597 20 68). M: Lima. Open Mon.-Fri. 9am-5:30pm. For reservations, call Mon.-Fri. 9am-6:30pm, Sat. 9am-3pm.
TWA: Pl. Colón, Torres de Colón (tel. 310 37 60). M: Colón. Open Mon.-Fri. 9am-5:30pm. For reservations, call Mon.-Fri. 9am-6pm.
British Airways: C. Serrano, 60 (tel. 431 75 75). M: Serrano. Open Mon.-Fri. 9am-5pm; tel. reservations Mon.-Fri. 9am-7pm.

By Train

Two *largo recorrido* (long distance) stations, **Atocha** and **Chamartín,** and two intermediate stations, **Recoletos** and **Nuevos Ministerios,** connect Madrid to the rest of the world. RENFE short-distance tickets can also be purchased and trains boarded at the following Metro stations: Embajadores, Méndez Alvaro, Laguna, Aluche, and Norte (access via extension from M: Ópera). Call RENFE (tel. 328 90 20) for reservations and the most reliable info.
RENFE Main Office, at C. Alcalá, 44, where Gran Vía hits C. Alcalá (M: Banco de España), is a useful place. Get national and international tickets here for departures from Chamartín. Schedules and AVE (Alta Velocidad Española) tickets are available (open Mon.-Fri. 9:30am-8pm).

Estación Chamartín: Agustín de Foxá (tel. 328 90 20 or 323 21 21). M: Chamartín. Bus #5 runs to and from Sol (45min.); the stop is just beyond the lockers. Ticket windows open 8:30am-10:30pm or 24hr. by phone. Chamartín services towns throughout Spain. International destinations include Lisbon and Paris. Most *cercanías* trains can be boarded here (see *Cercanías,* below). Chamartín has a tourist office, currency exchange, accommodations service, post office, telephones, car rental, lockers, bookstores, *cafeterías,* and police—not to mention a sports club and a roller-disco-bowl-a-rama upstairs.
Estación Atocha: (tel. 328 90 20 or 527 31 60). M: Atocha-Renfe. Ticket windows open 6:30am-11:30pm. Trains head south to provinces Andalucía, Castilla-La Mancha, Extremadura, and Valencia. Also services Salamanca, Portugal, El Escorial, and AVE service (tel. 534 05 05) to Sevilla via Córdoba. The cast-iron atrium of the original station has been turned into a simulated rainforest, making for a soothing, if humid, wait between trains.
Estación de Recoletos: Po. de Recoletos, 4. M: Colón. Entrance is on the middle segment of a split boulevard. Trains every 5-10min.
Estación Nuevos Ministerios: C. Raimundo Fernández Villaverde, on the corner with Po. Castellana. M: Nuevos Ministerios. Trains every 5-10min.

Cercanías (commuter trains) run to many popular destinations. Automatic ticket machines are in all *cercanía* stations. *Cercanías* are slow and make many stops. While some are modern and comfy, others lack A/C. However, *regional* or *regional-exprés* trains cost a bit more but go twice as fast—the *cercanía* fare to Ávila is 680ptas and the *regional-exprés* is only 785ptas.

By Bus

Numerous private companies, each with its own station and desti nations, serve Madrid, usually passing through the fume-ridden **Est ación Sur de Autobuses,** C. Canarias, E-16 (tel. 468 42 00 or 468 45 11). Part of the Palos de la Frontera Metro station, the Estación Sur is convenient for services and transport into the center of Madrid. Call from 7am to 11pm to make sure your destination is cov ered.

By Rideshare and Thumb

Auto Compartido, C. Carretas, 33, 3rd. fl. (24-hr. tel./fax 522 7 72), off Pta. del Sol. M: Sol, arranges shared journeys to destination in and out of Spain. Also check message boards at HI hostels, th TIVE travel agency, and English language bookstores for offers.

Hitchhiking is legal only on minor routes. The Guardia Civil d Tráfico picks up would-be highway and turnpike hitchhikers. Hitch hiking is not a recommended means of travel.

GETTING AROUND

Metro

Madrid has a fabulous Metro. Ten clean, efficient lines, referred t by color and number, connect Madrid's 126 stations. An individua Metro ticket costs 130ptas, but savvy riders opt for the *bonometr* (ticket of 10 rides) at 645ptas, or for a monthly pass. Remember t hold on to your ticket or pass until you leave the Metro—ridin without a receipt incurs an outrageous fine.

Trains run 6am-1:30am, not late enough (in Madrid time) to b deserted. Crime in the Metro stations is fairly rare, and women usu ally feel safe traveling alone. Do watch out for pickpocketin attempts in crowded cars. Some stations, particularly those con nected to two or more lines, have long tunnels and series of escala tors; exercise caution here and stick with people.

Bus

Unlike the Metro, bus transport provides you with a sense of dire tion and a scenic route. For guidance, check out the free *Madrid e Autobús* available at bus kiosks.

The fare is 130ptas and a 10-ride *bonobus* pass, sold at new stands and tobacco shops, costs 645ptas. Buses run from 6am-mid night. Between midnight and 3am, nocturnal buses travel from Sc and Pl. Cibeles to the outskirts every half-hour; after that, every hou until 5am. Nocturnal buses (numbered N1-N11) are listed on a spe cial section of the Plano.

Taxi

Zillions of taxis zip around Madrid at all hours. If you want to sum mon one to your door, call 445 90 08 or 447 51 80. The base fare 170ptas, plus 50-75ptas per km. Common fare additions include: t or from the airport (350ptas); to transport stations (150ptas); lu gage (50ptas per bag); Sundays and holidays (6am-11pm, 150ptas at night (11pm-6am, 150ptas). To the airport from the city cent costs about 2500ptas (cheaper from Pl. Colón, more from Sol).

Drivers do not generally cheat passengers; make sure, howeve that the driver turns on the meter. If you have a complaint or thin you've been overcharged, demand a *recibo oficial* (official receip and *hoja de reclamaciones* (complaint form), which the driver required to supply. Take down the license number, route taken, an fare charged. Drop off the forms and info at the City Hall, Pl. Villa, (tel. 447 07 15 or 447 07 14) to possibly get a refund.

To request taxi service for the **disabled,** call 547 82 00, 547 8 00, or 547 86 00; the rates are identical to those of other taxis.

congested traffic and nightmare parking doesn't unnerve you, sanely aggressive drivers, moped maniacs, and kamikaze pedestri-s will. Don't drive unless you're planning to zoom out of the city. To rent a car you must be over 21 and have an International river's License and major credit card (or· leave a deposit equal to e estimated rental fee). Gas isn't included in the price, and aver-es about 150ptas per liter. If renting for less than a week, you may be charged per kilometer. Tobacco shops sell parking permits.

Autos Bravo: C. Toledo, 136 (tel. 474 80 75). M: Puerta de Toledo. Medium-sized car 11,500ptas per day, 74,900ptas per week; insurance included; unlimited mileage (open Mon.-Fri. 9am-2pm and 4-8pm, Sat.-Sun. 9am-1pm).

Autos Viaducto: C. Segovia, 26 (tel. 548 48 48), C. Martín de los Heros, 23 (tel. 541 55 41), and Avda. Mediterráneo, 4 (tel. 433 12 33 or 552 10 44). Cheapest rates 5578ptas per day, including insurance; 100km free, then 17ptas per km after that. IVA not included. Open Mon.-Fri. 9am-1:30pm and 4-7:30pm.

OOD

eep in mind the following terms for quicker, cheaper fare: *boca-llo* (French bread sandwich, 350-400ptas); *sandwich* (sandwich n sliced bread, grilled, 300ptas); *croissant* (croissant sandwich, 50ptas); *ración* (large *tapa*, 300-500ptas). Fresh produce in adrid's center is scarce—try looking around a residential area for eighborhood markets. In general, *restaurantes* or *casas* are open om 1-4pm and 8pm-midnight; in the following listings, such is the se unless otherwise noted. More casual establishments such as *esones, cafeterías, bares, cafés, terrazas,* and *tabernas* serve rinks and food until midnight; some close on Sundays.

Groceries: %**Dia** and **Simago** are the cheapest city-wide super-market chains. **Mercado de San Miguel,** a charming covered market on Pl. San Miguel, is just off the northwest corner of Pl. Mayor (M: Sol), and there's a %**Dia** right behind it. Another cheap, covered market, **Mercado de la Cebada,** can be found at the intersection of C. Toledo and C. San Francisco (M: La Lat-ina; all open Mon.-Sat. 8am-2pm and 5:30-8pm). Every **El Corte Inglés** has an excellent food market (open Mon.-Sat. 10am-9pm).

Specialty Shops: Excellent pastry shops abound on Madrid's streets. The sublime **Horno La Santiaguesa,** C. Mayor, 73 (M: Sol), hawks everything from *roscones de reyes* (sweet bread for the Feast of the Epiphany) to chocolate and candy. **El Gourmet de Cuchilleros,** just through Pl. Mayor's Arco de Cuchilleros (M: Sol), is a gourmet store stocking lots of goodies.

Red Eye Establishments: *Guía del Ocio* lists late night eateries under *Cenar a Ultima Hora.* **VIPS,** Gran Vía, 43 (tel. 542 15 78; M: Callao), the deluxe version at C. Princesa, 5 (tel. 542 15 78; M: Ventura Rodríguez), or any of the other orange-sign branches around the city; and **BOB'S,** C. Serrano, 41 (M: Serrano), the green sign alternative, are two late-night options. (VIPS open daily 9am-3am; BOB'S open Sun.-Thurs. 9am-1:30am, Fri.-Sat. and evenings before holidays 9am-3am).

round Puerta del Sol and Plaza Mayor

hoose carefully, though you'll inevitably pay for the ambience. his area is overrun by tourists and prices for *típico* fare run steep.

Museo del Jamón, C. San Jerónimo, 6 (tel. 521 03 46). M: Sol. Five other locations throughout the city. If the pork perfume and in-your-face slabs of decorative meat rattle your nerves, head up to the dining room (opens at 1pm). Succulent Iberian ham serve■ in every form your piggish little heart could desire: *bocadill■ chiquito*, *ración* (100-600pta). Open Mon.-Sat. 9am-12:30am■ Sun. 10am-12:30am. Visa, AmEx.

Lhardy, C. San Jerónimo, 8 (tel. 521 33 85), at C. Victoria. M: S■ Circa 1839 dining at 2039 prices in one of Madrid's oldest resta■ rants—the 3600pta house specialty *cocido* is guarded by un■ formed men. Prime Minister Felipe González comes here o■ occasion for power lunches. Budget hounds congregate in th■ 1st-floor store for cognac, sherry, and the best hors d'oeuvres i■ town. Gourmet foodstuffs for sale. Open Mon.-Sat. 1-3:30pm an■ 9-11:30pm, Sun. 1-3:30pm. Visa, MC, AmEx.

Restaurante-Cafetería Sabatini, C. Bailén, 15 (tel. 547 9■ 40), opposite the Sabatini Gardens which are next to the Palac■ Real. M: Ópera. The sidewalk tables face some of Madrid's mo■ famous (and romantic) sights. Portly portions of *paella* or garl■ chicken (900ptas). Open 9am-1am. Dinner served 8pm-midnight■

Near Plaza Santa Ana

Plaza Santa Ana is lovely, shady, and less touristy than neighborin■ Puerta del Sol. **Calles Echegaray, Ventura de la Vega,** and **Mar■ uel Fernández González** are the budget boulevards.

Mesón La Caserola, C. Echegaray, 3 (tel. 429 39 63), off C. Sa■ Jerónimo. M: Sol. Bustling joint serves a solid *menú* (97■ 1500ptas) to ravenous locals. Try *tapas* in the raucous front are■ or dine in the *comedor* in back. A/C. Cheap *raciones* and *tapa■* during off-hours; entrees around 900ptas. Closes Mon. at noon.

Restaurante Integral Artemisa, C. Ventura de la Vega, 4 (te■ 429 50 92), off C. San Jerónimo. M: Sol. The most socially co■ scious restaurant in town—proceeds from Wed. dinners go t■ humanitarian organizations. Delicious cooking and no smokin■ Salads 750-1100ptas. Entrees 995-1350ptas. A/C. Visa.

Taberna D'a Quimada, C. Echegaray, 17 (tel. 429 32 63), on■ block down from C. San Jerónimo. M: Sol. A cauldron of *paell■* greets you at the door. *Menú* around 1000ptas. Entrees 80■ 1500ptas.

South of Puerta del Sol

The neighborhoods south of Sol, bounded by **Calles Atocha** an■ **Toledo,** are more residential and working class. No caviar here, b■ plenty of 1000pta *menús*. A la carte is often a better bargain.

El Granero de Lavapiés, C. Argumosa, 10 (tel. 467 76 11). ■ Lavapiés. Old world charm and new world food on a love■ street. Scrumptious carrot soup is just one vegetarian optio■ *Gazpacho* around 500ptas. *Menú* around 1100ptas. Open fo■ lunch Sun.-Fri. 1-4pm.

La Farfalla, C. Santa María, 17 (tel. 369 46 91). M: Antón Martí■ Their specialty is Argentine-style grilled meat, but true love is on■ unforgettable mouthful of their thin-crust pizza: *erótica* ■ *exquisita* 675ptas. Pastas 625-825ptas. Open for dinner Sun■ Thurs. until 3am; Fri.-Sat. until 4am.

Chueca

The none-too-closeted gay/glam district, where scenesters crow■ the chic gourmet joints and stalk the streets in platform shoes. Lo■ of good places to wine and dine, especially the former.

Nabucco, C. Hortaleza, 108 (tel. 410 06 11), a few blocks off P■ Santa Bárbara. M: Alonso Martínez or Chueca. Upscale clientel■ excellent food, and affordable prices. Pizzas 610-790ptas. Past■ 650-865ptas. Salads 370-755ptas. Visa, MC, AmEx, DC.

La Carreta, C. Barbieri, 10 (tel. 532 70 42 or 521 60 97), off C■ los Infantes. M: Gran Vía or Chueca. Specializes in Argentine, Ur■ guayan, and Chilean meals—lots of meat. Tango classes and pe■

formances are offered from 8:30pm-5am on weekends. *Menú* 1500ptas. Entrees 900ptas. *Menú* 1500ptas. Visa, MC, AmEx, DC.

Taberna Carmencita, C. San Marcos, 36, at C. Libertad. M: Chueca. Founded in 1830, this place evokes pre-War Madrid: brass fixtures, black and white photos of bullfighters, glazed tiles, iron and marble tables. *Menú* around 1300ptas plus 7% IVA. Excellent house wines. Entrees 900-2600ptas. Visa, MC, AmEx..

Malasaña

Streets radiating from Pl. 2 de Mayo drown in a sea of *cafeterías,* bars, restaurants, and pubs. **Calle San Andrés** is the most densely populated, but don't overlook **Calles San Bernardo** and **Manuela Malasaña.** Watch the colorful characters who fill the maze of tiny streets; watch them closely after dark.

La Gata Flora, C. Dos de Mayo, 1, and across the street at C. San Vicente Ferrer, 33 (tel. 521 20 20 or 521 27 92). M: Noviciado or Tribunal. Pizzas and pastas 875-1000ptas. Big, verdant salads 520-700ptas. Excellent *sangría* 900ptas. Open 2-6pm and 8:30pm-midnight; Fri.-Sat. open until 1:30am. Visa, MC, DC.

La Granja Restaurante Vegetariano, C. San Andrés, 11 (tel. 532 87 93), off Pl. 2 de Mayo. M: Tribunal. Candles and incense make for a romantic encounter of the vegetarian kind. Salads around 700ptas. Entrees (including *arroz con algas*—rice with seaweed) 600-750ptas. Lunch *menú* 900ptas. Closed Tues. Visa.

El Restaurante Vegetariano, C. Marqués de Santa Ana, 34, off Pl. Juan Pujol on the corner with C. Espíritu Santo. M: Tribunal. Another sanctuary for vegetarians, though smaller and a tad pricier than La Granja. Homemade bread. Soups 500ptas. Salad bar 550-775ptas. Main dishes 1000ptas. Closed Mon. Visa, MC.

Beyond Bilbao

The area north of Glorieta de Bilbao (M: Bilbao) in the V formed by **Calles Fuencarral** and **Luchana,** and including **Plaza Olavide,** is swarming with bars, clubs, cafés, and restaurants.

La Tarterie, C. Cardenal Cisneros, 24 (tel. 447 05 54), right off C. Luchana, which is off Glorieta de Bilbao. M: Bilbao. This restaurant/art gallery features temporary exhibits, mostly experimental. Packed with struggling artists and quiche connoisseurs. Great quiches, salads, and pizzas (600-1100ptas).

Pizza Buona, C. Hartzenbusch, 19 (tel. 448 23 87), off C. Cardenal Cisneros, which is right off C. Luchana. M: Bilbao. A patriotic green, red, and white decorated Italian restaurant on a German-named street in the heart of Spain. Tasty pizzas 525-790ptas. A/C.

Bar Samara, C. Cardenal Cisneros, 13. M: Bilbao. Bills itself as Egyptian, but offers Middle Eastern staples. Hummus, *baba ganoush,* and *tahini* salads 475-525ptas. Kabobs and other entrees from 1500ptas. Gets crowded after dark. A/C. Open Sun.-Thurs. until midnight, Fri.-Sat. until 1am. Closed Mon.

Argüelles

Argüelles is a middle-class *barrio* near the Ciudad Universitaria, full of student-priced eateries and neighborhood bars.

Cáscaras, C. Ventura Rodríguez, 7 (tel. 542 83 36). M: Ventura Rodríguez. This slick and affordable restaurant demonstrates the creative potential of the *tortilla.* Vegetarian dishes 675-975ptas. *Tortillas* 745-955ptas. Salads 675-850ptas.

La Crêperie, Po. Pintor Rosales, 28 (tel. 548 23 58). M: Ventura Rodríguez. Affordable crêpes on the chic Po. Rosales. Colorful, cupid-centered menus for twentysomething clientele. Salty crêpes 515-670ptas. Dessert crepes 360-625ptas. Coffee 135ptas. Open Sun.-Thurs. until 1am, Fri.-Sat. until 1:30am.

Tapas

Hopping from bar to bar gobbling *tapas* is an active alternative to
sit-down meal. Most *tapas* bars *(tascas* or *tabernas)* are open no
to 4pm and 8pm to midnight or later. Some, doubling as restauran
cluster around **Plaza Mayor** (tourist alert!) and **Plaza Santa An**

La Toscana, C. Manuel Fernández González, 10-17 (tel. 429
31). On the corner with C. Ventura de la Vega. M: Sol. A friend
mesón with crockery dangling from the woodwork. Beautif
tapas. Often jam-packed on weekends. Open Thurs.-Tues. noc
4pm and 8pm-midnight.

La Trucha, C. Nuñez de Arce, 6 (tel. 532 08 82). M: Sol. Cramp
but cheap, and popular with locals. Open Mon.-Sat. 12:30-4p
and 8pm-midnight.

El Anciano Rey de los Vinos, C. Bailén, 19 (tel. 248 50 52),
block from where C. Mayor hits C. Bailén. M: Sol. A bright, lof
ceilinged bar, with cider on tap and a wide selection of hou
wines. Open 10am-3pm and 5:30-11:30pm. Closed Wed.

La Chuleta, C. Echegaray, 20 (tel. 429 37 29). Spacious and mc
ern. Savory *tortillas, calamares* (squid), and peppers. Open Su
Tues., Thurs. noon-1am, Fri.-Sat. noon-3am. AmEx and travele
checks accepted.

ENTERTAINMENT AND NIGHTLIFE

The **Guía del Ocio** (125ptas) should be your first purchase
Madrid. This weekly entertainment paper tells you what's in: cc
certs, exhibits, cinema, restaurants, bars, clubs, and sports are
listed. The *Guía,* available behind the counter of any kiosk, com
out on Thursday or Friday for the following week.

Spaniards get an average of one less hour of sleep than other Eur
peans. People in Madrid claim to need even less than that. Enc
mously proud of their nightlife (they'll tell you with a straight fa
that they were bored in Paris or New York), *madrileños* insist th
no one goes to bed until they've killed the night—and a good part
the following morning.

Plaza 2 de Mayo (#16; D8) in Malasaña, **Plaza Chueca, Pla**
de España, and the **Gran Vía** can be intimidating and sleaz
Madrid is fairly safe for a city of its size, but one should always exe
cise caution. The only really fearsome places late at night are th
parks.

As the sun sets and bathes the streets in gold during the summe
terrazas (or **chiringuitos,** outdoor cafés) sprawl across sidewal
all over Madrid. Colder weather sends *madrileños* scrambling in
packed bars and discotecas. In addition to our specific listings, th
following neighborhoods are good places to explore.

Plaza Mayor: Flocking with tourists and pigeons, but handy for
(pricey) beer or glass of wine while digesting tourist brochures

Plaza de Chueca: *Terrazas* face popular clubs, brimming wi
the artsy and hip. Several gay and lesbian bars and cafés.

Parque del Retiro: Outdoor kiosks and bars. After sundow
only the north gate stays open. Don't wander alone after dark.

Plaza 2 de Mayo (Malasaña) and **Plaza Olavide** (Bilbao): We
dressed twentysomethings quaff drinks in the shade.

Paseos Castellana, Recoletos, and **Prado:** Fashionable and
bit pricey. La Castellana showcases model types and money-ma
ers.

El Viso: Between Po. Castellana and C. María de Molina. A pre-w
garden city within the city. Villas, walled gardens, and windi
streets with *terrazas* exude a charming village-like aura.

Bars

Bocaccio, Po. Castellana, 21. An ultra-fashionable *terraza* and great place to people-watch. Forget about finding a place to sit. Open daily noon-3am.

Naturbier, Pl. Santa Ana, 9 (tel. 429 39 18). M: Antón Martín. Has a superior *lager* for 225-260ptas. Open Sun.-Thurs. 11am-12am, Fri.-Sat. 11am-3am.

Chapandaz, C. Fernando Católico, 1 block from Arcipreste de Hita, down the stairs to the right. M: Moncloa. Strip mall by day, raging student hub by night. Near several bars, but only Chapandaz has stalactites and the mysterious *leche de pantera* (panther's milk). Large mixed drinks 500ptas. Open until 2am.

Live Music and Jazz Clubs

Manuela, C. San Vicente Ferrer, 29 (tel. 531 70 37). M: Tribunal Elegant and mirrored café bar. Live music (usually folksy) begins at 11:30pm; cover 300-400ptas. Open nightly 7pm-3am.

Cambalache, C. San Lorenzo, 5 (tel. 310 07 01). M: Alonso Martínez or Tribunal. Live tangos, Argentine food, and drinks at the bar from 6-11pm. Consider reserving ahead. Open 8:30pm-5am.

Café Jazz Populart, C. Huertas, 22 (tel. 429 84 07). M: Antón Martín. Serious jazz aficionados in a classy, smoky bar. Live music Fri.-Wed.: jazz, blues, swing, reggae, flamenco, and Latin jazz. No cover. Pitcher of beer 300ptas, but all prices double during performances (11pm and 12:30pm). Open 6pm-3am.

Clamores Jazz Club, C. Albuquerque, 14 (tel. 445 79 38), off C. Cardenal Cisneros. M: Bilbao. Swanky setting and the best jazz Madrid has to offer. The cover (600ptas) gets slipped into the bill. Drink prices double during performances (600-1200ptas). Live jazz Tues.-Sun. Open 7pm-3am. Fri. and Sat. until 4am.

Dance Clubs

For **clubs and discos,** life begins around 2am. Many discos have "afternoon" sessions (usually 7-10pm, cover 250-1000ptas) for teens; but the "night" sessions (lasting until dawn) are when to really let your hair down. The *entrada* (cover; often includes a drink) can be as high as 2000ptas, and men may be charged up to 500ptas more than women. Keep an eye out for *invitaciones* and *oferta* cards—in stores, restaurants, or handed out in the streets—that offer discounts or free admission.

Club Andy Warhol's, C. Luchana, 20. M: Bilbao. Wait…is that a Warhol print? or the person I'm dancing with? By the time you make it to this chic disco, you'll be seeing in multiples. Open 5am (yup, am)-around 10am, Sun. 5am-noon.

Joy Eslava, C. Arenal, 11 (tel. 366 37 33). M: Sol or Ópera. A 3-tiered theater turned disco; 3 bars, laser lights, live entertainment. Cover 1500ptas, includes one drink. Open Mon.-Thurs. 11:30pm on, Fri.-Sat. 7-10:15pm and 11:30pm-5:30am.

Ya'sta, C. Valverde, 10. M: Gran Vía. Punk and grunge until the wee hours in this new club. Cover 5000ptas. Open Sun.-Thurs. 8pm-1:30am, Fri.-Sat. 8pm-8am.

Vía Láctea, C. Verlarde, 18 (tel. 466 75 81). M: Tribunal. Jam-packed and deservedly famous. Open Tues.-Sun 7pm-3:30am.

Révolver, C. Galileo, 26 (tel. 594 26 79). M: Argüelles. Large club hosts a variety of concerts and special events. Call for details and current schedule. Cover 700-2000ptas, depending on the event.

Angels of Xenon, C. Atocha, 38 (tel. 369 38 81). M: Antón Martín. The place to be, but almost too cool for the likes of you. 1000pta cover includes one drink.

Gay & Lesbian Clubs

El Mosquito, Torrecilla de Leal, 13. M: Antón Martín. Rap, soul, and funk draw a lesbian and gay crowd. Drinks 300-700ptas. Open Sun.-Thurs. 6pm-12:30am, Fri.-Sat. 6pm-3am.

Acuarela, C. Gravina, 8, off C. Hortaleza. M: Chueca. Artsy caf
offers an alternative to cruising. High flesh to space ratio.

Truco, C. Gravina, 10 (tel. 532 89 21). M. Chueca. Classy bar, fe
turing local artists' work. Lesbian friendly.

Theater

In July and August, **Plaza Mayor, Plaza de Lavapiés, Plaza Vill**
de París, and other meeting places host frequent plays. Buy ticke
at theater box offices or at agencies. The theater district is bounde
by Pl. Santa Ana and Pl. Colón (south-north) and Po. Prado-Recole
tos and Pta. del Sol (east-west). The state-run theaters and many o
the private theaters are sights in themselves.

Centro Cultural de la Villa, Pl. Colón (tel. 575 60 80). M
Colón or Serrano. A major city-run center. Tickets 2000ptas.

Sala Olimpia, C. Valencia (tel. 527 46 22). M: Lapiés. Nationa
troupe produces avant-garde theatrical works. Tickets 220
2500ptas; ask about student discounts.

Teatro Español, C. Príncipe, 25 (tel. 429 62 97). M: Sol. Site o
16th-century Teatro de Príncipe, the Teatro Español dates from
the 18th century. Established company run by city hall regularl
showcases winners of the prestigious Lope de Vega award. Tick
ets 200-2000ptas. 50% discount on Wed. Excellent, traditiona
Café del Príncipe inside.

Film

In summer, the city sponsors free movies and plays which are liste
in the *Guía del Ocio* and the entertainment supplements in Frida
papers. Most cinemas have three showings per day at around 4:3(
7:30, and 10:30pm. Tickets are 600-700ptas. Some cinemas offe
matinee student discounts for 400ptas. Wednesday is *día del esp*
ctador: tickets are 400-500ptas for the matinée—show up early.

Subtitled films are shown in many private theaters, includin
Alphaville (tel. 559 38 36; M: Plaza de España), **Multicines Idea**
(tel. 369 25 18; M: Sol), **Princesa** (tel. 559 98 72; M: Plaza d
España), and **Renoir I** (tel. 559 57 60; M: Plaza de España) and
(tel. 534 00 77; M: Cuatro Caminos). Check the *versión origina*
(V.O.) listings in entertainment guides. The state-subsidized *filme*
teca in the renovated Art Deco **Ciné Doré,** C. Santa Isabel, 3 (te
369 11 25; M: Antón Martín), is the best for repertory cinema (tick
ets 200-400ptas). It also has a bar, restaurant, and bookstore. Th
Centro Reina Sofía has a repertory cinema of its own. **Gran Ví**
is lined with plush cinemas.

Flamenco

Flamenco in Madrid is tourist-oriented and expensive.

Café de Chinitas, C. Torija, 7 (tel. 547 15 01 or 547 15 02; M
Santo Domingo), is as ostentatious and flamboyant as they come
The show starts at 10:30pm and midnight; the memories last for
ever (they'd better). The 4200pta cover includes one drink.

Corral de la Morería, C. Morería, 17 (tel. 365 84 46 or 365 1
37; M: La Latina), by the Viaducto on C. Bailén, shows start a
10:45 and last till 2am. The 4000pta cover includes one drink.

Casa Patas, C. Ceñizares, 10 (tel. 369 04 96; M: Antón Martín), i
a more down-to-earth flamenco club. Shows start at midnight on
Thurs.-Sat. nights. Cover varies (open Mon.-Sat. 8pm-2:30am).

Classical Music

Auditorio Nacional (#3; A3), C. Príncipe de Vergara, 136 (te
337 01 00; M: Cruz del Rayo), hosts the finest classical perfor
mances. Home to the Orquesta Nacional, it has a magnificent ha
for symphonic music and a smaller one for chamber recitals.

Conservatorio Superior de Música, recently moved into the
18th-century medical building next door to the Centro Reina

Sofía, hosts free student performances, professional traveling orchestras, and celebrated soloists.

La Corrida (The Bullfight)

Corridas (bullfights) are held during the Festival of San Isidro and every Sunday in summer, less frequently the rest of the year. The season lasts from March to October, signalled by posters in bars and cafés (especially on C. Victoria, off C. San Jerónimo).

Plaza de las Ventas, C. Alcalá, 237 (tel. 356 22 00; M: Ventas), east of central Madrid, is the biggest ring in Spain. Metro or bus rides, even 1½hr. before the fight, can be asphyxiating. A seat is 450-15,200ptas, depending on its location either in the *sombra* (shade) or the blistering *sol.* Tickets are usually available the Friday and Saturday before and the Sunday of the bullfight.

Museo Taurino, C. Alcalá, 237 (tel. 725 18 57), at Pl. Monumental de Las Ventas. For those intrigued by the lore, not the gore. The museum displays a remarkable collection of *trajes de luces,* capes, and posters of famous *corridas.* (Open Mon.-Fri. 9:30am-2:30pm. On fight days it opens 1hr. before the *lidia.* Free.)

Sports

Spanish sports fans obsess over **fútbol** (soccer). If either one of the two big local teams, Real Madrid or Atlético Madrid, wins a match, count on streets being clogged with screaming fans and honking cars. Every Sunday and some Saturdays between September and June, one of these two teams plays at home. Real Madrid plays at **Estadio Santiago Bernabéu,** Po. Castellana, 104 (tel. 457 11 12; M: Lima). Atlético de Madrid plays at **Estadio Vicente Calderón,** C. Virgen del Puerto, 67 (tel. 366 47 07; M: Pirámides or Marqués de Vadillos). Tickets for seats cost 2500ptas, for standing 1000ptas. Scalpers lurk around the stadium during the afternoon or evening a few days before the game. These tickets cost only 25-50% more, whereas on game day prices become astronomical.

El Rastro, Flea Market Extraordinaire

Every Sunday morning for hundreds of years, **El Rastro** has been *the* place to sell stolen watches and buy battered birdcages. Old shoes, tacky clothes, and cheap jewelry abound, but the intrepid shopper will find good deals on second-hand leather jackets, leather bags, and canaries (on their own special sidestreet). Antiquarians lend their peculiar mustiness to Calle (not Salón or Paseo) del Prado and adjacent streets. From Pl. Mayor, walk down C. Toledo to Pl. Cascorro (M: La Latina), where the market begins, and follow the rest of the world downhill to the end, at the bottom of C. Ribera de Curtidores. To avoid the crowd, arrive no later than 10am and drift off to an air-conditioned bar when the sun goes vertical (Los Caracoles is convenient; see *Tapas,* p. 10). Enormously crowded, the flea market is a den of pickpockets, so wear your backpack backwards (that is, frontwards), and be very discreet when taking out your wallet or money. (Market open Sun. and holidays 9am-2pm.)

MUSEUMS

El Triángulo del Arte

Museo del Prado (#69; C14-15; tel. 420 28 36), Po. Prado at Pl. Cánovas del Castillo (M: Banco de España or Atocha). Spain's premier museum and one of Europe's finest, the Neoclassical building has sheltered the royal painting collection since the time of Fernando VII. The Prado's collection of over 3000 paintings includes Spanish and foreign masterpieces, with particular strengths in the Flemish and Venetian Schools. Open Tues.-Sat. 9am-7pm, Sun. 9am-2pm. Admission including the Casón del Buen Retiro (see below) 400ptas, students 200ptas. *Paseo del*

Arte ticket (includes Prado, Thyssen, and Reina Sofía) 1050ptas. Free Sat. 2:30-7pm and Sun. 9am-2pm. With your ticket stub from the Prado, walk 3min. from the Prado to C. Alfonso XXII, 28 (tel. 468 04 81), facing the Parque de Retiro. Once part of Felipe IV's Palacio del Buen Retiro, the **Casón del Buen Retiro** (#63, B15) was destroyed in the war against Napoleon. It now has a superb collection of 19th-century Spanish paintings. Enter the *Sección de Arte Español del Siglo XIX* from the side. Open Tues.-Sat. 9am-6:45pm, Sun. 9am-1:45pm.

Museo Nacional Centro de Arte Reina Sofía (#80; C14; tel. 467 50 62), C. Santa Isabel, 52, opposite Estación Atocha at the south end of Po. del Prado (M: Atocha). A marvelous permanent collection of 20th-century art, including Picasso's tour de force *Guernica,* occupies two floors in this recently renovated museum. Three floors contain rotating exhibits, library and archives specializing in 20th-century art (open Mon. and Wed.-Fri. 10am-9pm), photography archives, music library, repertory cinema (art films in Spanish at noon and 4:30pm, 150ptas), café, and a flashy gift shop. Open Mon., Wed.-Sat. 10am-9pm, Sun. 10am-2:30pm. 400ptas, students 200ptas. Free Sun., and Sat. after 2:30pm.

Museo Thyssen-Bornemisza (#52; B14; tel. 369 01 51), at the corner of Po. Prado and C. San Jerónimo, just up the street from the Prado (M: Banco de España). This beautiful museum houses the fabulous and newly purchased (June, 1993) 775-piece Thyssen-Bornemisza collection. An 18th-century palace rehabilitated by Moneo, the Thyssen provides a survey course in art history. Almost all the great names of the 20th century are represented, and other attractions include impressionist, post-impressionist, Fauvist, and expressionist works, as well as 17th-century Dutch paintings, 18th-century Rococo, and 19th-century Romanticism and realism. Open Tues.-Sun. 10am-7pm. No one admitted after 6:30pm. 600ptas, students with ISIC and retired people 350ptas, children under 12 free.

Others

Convento de las Descalzas Reales (#37; A17, B13), Pl. Descalzas (tel. 521 27 79), between Pl. Callao and Sol. M: Callao or Sol. Originally a palace inhabited by the royal family of Castile, this convent, still in operation today, was founded as such in 1559. The museum holds canvases by Zurbarán, Titian, and Rubens. Visitors are taken on a guided tour conducted in Spanish (about 45min; a wait is sometimes necessary). Open Tues.-Thurs. and Sat. 10:30am-1pm and 4-6pm, Fri. 10:30am-1pm, Sun. 11am-2pm. 650ptas, students 250ptas. Convent's church free during mass (Mon.-Sat. 8am and 7pm, Sun. 8am and noon).

Convento de la Encarnación (#33; A12), in Pl. Encarnación (tel. 542 00 59), off C. Bailén near and east of the Palacio Real. M: Ópera. A lovely convent, but not as impressive as the Convento de las Descalzas Reales. The fascinatingly macabre *relicuario* houses about 1500 relics of saints, including a vial of San Pantaleón's blood, believed to liquefy every year on July 27. In one recent year, 30,000 people showed up to gawk. Open Wed. and Sat. 10:30am-12:30pm and 4-5:30pm, Sun. 11am-1:30pm. 600ptas, students 200ptas.

Museo Cerralbo (#24; A12), C. Ventura Rodríguez, 17 (tel. 547 36 46). M: Ventura Rodríguez. Once home to the Marquis of Cerralbo XVII (1845-1922), this palatial residence-turned-museum displays an eclectic assemblage of period furniture and ornamentation. Beautiful Venetian glass chandeliers and a so-called "mysterious" clock by Barbedienne stand out. Open Tues.-Sat. 9:30am-2:30pm, Sun. 10am-2pm. 400ptas, students 200ptas. Free on Wed. and Sun.

Museo de América, Av. Reyes Católicos, 6, near Av. Puerta de Hierro and north of the C. Princesa junction, next to the futuristic metal tower (tel. 544 67 42). M: Moncloa. This fantastic museum documents the societies and cultures of pre-Columbian civilizations of the Americas, as well as the Spanish conquest. Renovated to include state-of-the-art multimedia exhibits. Open Tues.-Sat. 10am-3pm, Sun. 10am-2:30pm. 400ptas, students 200ptas.

Museo de la Real Academia de Bellas Artes de San Fernando (#41; A18, B13), C. Alcalá, 13 (tel. 522 14 91). M: Sol or Sevilla. A beautiful museum with an excellent collection of Old Masters surpassed only by the Prado. Masterpieces include Velázquez's portraits of Felipe IV and Mariana de Austria and Goya's *La Tirana*. Other notable works are the Italian Baroque collection, 17th-century canvases by Ribera, Murillo, and Zurbarán, and a large collection of Picasso prints. Open July 16-Sept. 15 9am-3pm; otherwise Tues.-Fri. 9am-7pm, Sat.-Mon. 9am-12:30pm. 200ptas, students 100ptas, free Sat. and Sun. The **Calcografía Real** (Royal Print and Drawing Collection) in the same building houses Goya's studio. Free with museum admission.

Museo Arqueológico Nacional (#26; A15), C. Serrano, 13 (tel. 577 79 12), behind the *Biblioteca Nacional*. M: Serrano. Travel back in time to the Middle Ages, Ancient Greece and Egypt, the Stone Age...the history of the entire western world is on display in this huge museum. Parts of the museum are sometimes closed; call ahead. Open Tues.-Sat. 9:30am-8:30pm, Sun. 9:30am-2:30pm. 400ptas, students 200ptas. Free on Sun.

Museo Lázaro Galdiano (#13; C10), C. Serrano, 122 (tel. 561 60 84). M: Rubén Dario. The beautiful, ornate building alone makes this museum worth a visit. Displays a wide array of paintings, Italian Renaissance bronzes, ancient jewels, Gothic reliquaries, and Celtic and Visigoth brasses. Open Sept.-July Tues.-Sun. 10am-2pm. 300ptas.

Museo Sorolla (#14; C9), Po. General Martínez Campos, 37 (tel. 410 15 84). M: Rubén Darío or Iglesia. Former home and studio of Joaquín Sorolla, the acclaimed 19th-century Valencian painter. Sorolla's seaside paintings and tranquil garden make for a refreshing break from other crowded museums. Open Sept.-July Tues.-Sun. 10am-2pm. 400ptas, students 200ptas.

SIGHTS

To visit Madrid and not stroll from the Puerta del Sol to the Paseo del Prado and the Plaza Mayor to the Palacio Real would be as tragic as bypassing the sights themselves. Madrid, large as it may seem, is a walker's city. Sights are listed here by geographical location. The grand scheme is roughly semicircular: we begin in the medieval-Habsburg heart of the city, and then travel successively east, north, and west, concluding with El Pardo.

From Plaza Mayor to Puerta de Toledo

Plaza Mayor (#60; B17, B13; M: Sol), an easy orientation point for any walking expedition through Madrid. An elegant arcaded square, topped with the Habsburgs' black slate roofs and spindly, pagoda-like towers, once the site of bullfights and public executions. The plaza was completed in 1620 for Felipe III; his statue graces its center. As soon as the sun begins its descent, *madrileños* emerge, tourists multiply, and café tables fill with lively patrons. Every Sunday morning, collectors assemble at the **coin and stamp market** (open 8am-2pm). During the annual **Fiesta de San Isidro** (May 15-22), the Plaza explodes in boisterous festivity. The surrounding streets, especially those through the **Arco de los Cuchilleros** on the southwest corner of the Plaza, house old specialty shops and renowned *mesones*.

Plaza Santa Cruz (#61; B13, B18), just east of Pl. Mayor via C. Zaragoza (M: Sol). A tranquil plaza and site of the **Palacio de Santa Cruz** (#65; B13, B18). Formerly a prison, the palace exemplifies the Habsburg style with its alternation of red brick and granite corners and black-slate towers.

Iglesia de San Isidro (#75; B18), south of Pl. Mayor on C. Toledo (M: Latina). The 17th-century church was designed by

Sanchez and Bautista and restored after the interior was burned by rioting workers in 1936. The remains of San Isidro landed here after being tossed from church to church. Open for mass only.

Iglesia de San Andrés and **Capilla de San Isidro** (#74; C12, C17), C. San Andrés (M: Latina). Inside the Baroque red brick and granite *iglesia* is a magnificently carved polychrome altarpiece by Francisco Giralte. Open for mass only.

Plaza de la Paja (#72; C17), Madrid's erstwhile main square, up C. San Andrés (M: Latina). The imposing and elaborate Renaissance **Capilla del Obispo** (#73; C12, C17) dominates the plaza.

Plaza San Francisco (#76; D12, D17) and **Iglesia de San Francisco el Grande** (St. Francis of Assisi; #77; D17), Carrera San Francisco (M: Puerta de Toledo or Latina). One of the most impressive examples of Bourbon Neoclassicism. Open in summer Tues.-Sat. 11am-1pm and 5-8pm. St. Francis himself allegedly built a convent next door in the 13th century, where the **Capilla de Cristo de los Dolores** sits today.

Puente de Toledo, spanning the **Río Manzanares,** Madrid's notoriously dinky river (M: Pirámides). The broad Baroque bridge makes up for the river's aesthetic inadequacies. Sandstone carvings on one side of the bridge depict San Isidro rescuing his son from a well, and his wife Santa María de la Cabeza on the other.

Puente de Segovia (#70; B11), the Renaissance bridge which fords the river from C. Segovia. Conceived by Juan de Herrera, the talented designer of El Escorial. Both bridges afford gorgeous views (and fertile ground for the blossoming of young love).

Paseos Prado, Recoletos, and Castellana

Paseo Prado-Recoletos, running from Estación Atocha to Plaza Colón, is one of the great European ensembles of Neoclassical and revival architecture. With virtually every major museum in the vicinity, this "museum mile" is the veritable cultural axis of Madrid. The **Palacio de Buenavista** (#29; A14; atop a slope overlooking Pl. Cibeles), the **Banco de España** (#39; B14), and the second-hand bookstalls on the **Cuesta de Moyano** also line the avenue. Paseo Castellana holds many of the magnificent apartment buildings and mansions belonging to aristocrats before the war. Although a number were torn down in the 60s, some of the buildings that replaced the originals are boldly imaginative; the juxtaposition of new and old money is striking.

Ministerio de Agricultura, just southwest of Retiro, on Glorieta de Atocha (M: Atocha). This imposing, ceramic-decked building was built by Ricardo Velázquez in the 1880s. The stone creatures on top of the building represent industry and commerce.

Iglesia de San Jerónimo (#68; B15), behind the Prado (M: Atocha). This church was built by Hieronymite monks and re-endowed by the Catholic monarchs. It has witnessed many a joyous milestone: Fernando and Isabel were crowned and King Alfonso XIII married here (open 6am-1pm and 6-8pm).

Academia Española (#62; B15), bastion of great minds and Spanish culture, also sits behind the Prado.

Obelisco a los Mártires del 2 de Mayo, in Pl. Lealtad (M: Banco de España), is filled with the ashes of those who died in the 1808 uprising against Napoleon. Behind the memorial sits the gracefully colonnaded **Bolsa de Madrid** (stock exchange; #46; B15). The **Fuente de Apollo,** one of three aquatic masterpieces along this avenue, sprays solemnly.

Fuente de la Cibeles (#34; B14), in front of the extravagant **Palacio de Comunicaciones** (#40; B15; M: Banco de España), the central post office, depicts the fertility goddess's triumphant arrival in a carriage drawn by lions. Madrid residents protected this emblem of their city during Franco's bomb raids by covering it with sandbags.

Casa de América (#30; A15), on the northeastern corner of the intersection, was formerly the Palacio de Linares, a 19th-century townhouse built for Madrid nobility (M: Banco de España). Long abandoned by its former residents and proved by a team of "scientists" to be inhabited by ghosts, it was transformed into a library and lecture halls for the study of Latin American culture and politics. It sponsors art exhibitions, guest lectures, and tours of the palace.

Biblioteca Nacional (#22; A15), 20 Po. Prado (M: Colón), exhibits treasures from the collections of various monarchs. Has many historic manuscripts, including a first-edition copy of *Don Quijote*.

Plaza Colón (#18; A15), where jetlagged moles emerge from underground (where the Bus-Aeropuerto drops off) in the **Jardines del Descubrimiento** (Gardens of Discovery; #19; A15; M: Colón). Huge clay boulders loom at one side, inscribed with odd trivia about the New World, including Seneca's prediction of the discovery, the names of mariners on board the caravels, and quotes from Columbus's diary.

Centro Cultural de la Villa (#18; A15; tel. 575 60 80), below the gardens of the plaza, hosts concerts, lectures, ballet, and plays. On its front, facing a noisy waterfall, a map details the explorer's voyages. A more traditional monument to Columbus stands directly above the Centro Cultural.

Estadio Santiago Bernabéu (#2; A3), Plaza de Lima (M: Nuevos Ministerios or Cuzco), past the Picasso and Europa Towers. This squat stadium hosts the Real Madrid *fútbol* team.

Puerta de Europa (#1; A2), a colossal structure that can be seen from the stadium (M: Pl. Castilla), gives fans of modern skyscraper architecture goosebumps.

Between Sol and Paseo del Prado

Puerta del Sol (#50; A18, B13), an intersection of eight major streets (M: Sol). The "Kilometro 0" marker on the sidewalk in front of the 18th-century **Casa de Correos** (now the police headquarters) signals Madrid's epicenter. Sol is the transportation hub of the city and is packed with restaurants, shops, tourists, banks, hostels, and services of all kinds. In the middle of the square, a statue of a bear hugs an arbutus tree, the city's coat of arms *(el oso y el madroño)*. The Puerta del Sol witnessed one of the most resonant moments in Spanish history, when *madrileños* rose up against Napoleon's army after learning of his plan to remove the Royal Infantas. Two of Goya's paintings in the Prado, *El dos de mayo* (May 2, 1908) and *Los fusilamientos del tres de mayo* (The Execution of the Rioters: May 3, 1808), depict the episode.

Iglesia de las Calatravas (#38; B14), C. Alcalá, 25 (M: Sevilla), is what remains of the huge Convento de la Concepción Real de Comendadoras. Pablo González Velázquez's Baroque altarpiece contrasts with the building's stark Renaissance exterior. Artisans designed a unique ornamental cross motif now named after this church (open for mass only, 7:30am-1pm and 6-8pm). Madrid's cultural elite can be spotted schmoozing at the **Círculo de Bellas Artes** across the street.

Palacio Miraflores, Cra. San Jerónimo, 19 (M: Sevilla), was designed by the premier 18th-century architect Pedro de Ribera. Ribera's **Palacio del Marqés de Ugena** is at C. Príncipe, 28, off of Cra. San Jerónimo on your left.

Plaza Santa Ana (#66; B13), following C. Príncipe downhill (M: Sol). The enchanting, shady plaza has a hopping bar and café scene.

Ateneo Científico y Literario de Madrid (#51; B14), C. del Prado (tel. 429 17 56), on the southeast side of the plaza. Long a focal point in the cultural life of the city and a hangout for Madrid's intellectuals, the Ateneo is now mainly a private library. Its evening concerts and symposia are often open to the public.

Real Academia de la Historia (#41; A18, B13), where C. Huertas meets C. León (M: Antón Martín), houses a magnificent old library of its own. This area has been literary since Spain's Golden Age: Cervantes, Góngora, Quevedo, Calderón, Moratín, and others lived and pontificated here.

The Retiro and Jerónimos

The delightful, pastoral, 300-acre **Parque del Retiro** (#47; B15; M: Retiro) was originally intended to be a *buen retiro* (nice retreat) for Felipe IV. Today the Retiro is Madrid's top picnic and suntanning zone. The northeast corner of the park swells with monastery ruins and waterfalls. At nightfall during the summer (when only the north gate remains open), Retiro becomes a lively bar and café hangout, but avoid venturing into the park alone after dark.

Estanque Grande (#48; B16), a rectangular lake in the middle of the park, has been the social center of the Retiro ever since aspiring caricaturists, tarot card readers, Michael Jackson impersonators, and sunflower seed vendors parked their goods along its marble shore. Boat rentals are available here (9:30am-8:30pm, cool paddle boats 550ptas for 4 people, less cool motorboat 150ptas per person).

Palacio de Cristal (#71; B16), south of the lake, was built as an exhibit hall for Philippine flowers. The Palacio now hosts a variety of art shows. Open Tues.-Sat. 11am-2pm and 5-8pm, Sun. 10am-2pm. Admission varies, but often free. May be closed for repairs.

Palacio de Velázquez (#64; B16; named after the architect, not the artist), an impressive exhibit hall, works in conjunction with the Museo de Arte Reina Sofía.

Puerta de Alcalá (#31; A15), at Pl. Independencia, is permanently scarred by Civil War bullets. Revenue from an unpopular wine tax paid for this imposing Neoclassical arch honoring Carlos III in 1778.

Observatorio Astronómico (#81; C15), south of Retiro on Av. Alfonso XII, is at the summit of a grassy slope. Villanueva's 18th-century structure is considered one of the most elegant examples of Spanish Neoclassicism. Open Mon.-Fri. 9am-2pm.

Jardín Botánico (#78; C15), north of the Observatorio, on Po. Prado, is lush and shady with imported trees, bushes, and flowers from occident to orient. Open 10am-9pm; in winter 10am-7pm; in spring and fall 10am-8pm. 200ptas, students 100ptas.

Around the Gran Vía

Narrow C. Barquillo, the main throughfare of the Pl. Salesas district, is yet another microcosm of Madrid-style architecture. It's off the west end of the Gran Vía, near M: Banco de España.

Iglesia de las Salesas Reales, at Pl. Salesas (M: Colón). Commissioned by Bourbon King Fernando VI at the request of his wife Doña Bárbara in 1758, the Baroque-Neoclassical domed church is clad in granite, with façade sculptures by Alfonso Vergaza and dome painting by the brothers González Velázquez. The ostentatious façade and interior prompted critics to pun on the queen's name: "Barbaric queen, barbaric tastes, barbaric building, barbarous expense." The royal couple is buried here.

Plaza de España (#25; A12), at the end of Gran Vía (M: Pl. España). This area has been called the Franco regime's very own plaza. It was laid out in the 1940s and is flanked by two classic regime-sponsored buildings: the 50s-modern **Torre Madrid** (#27; A12) and the huge **Edificio España** (#28; A12; café on the 26th floor open noon to early evening; 100pta cover).

Monument to Cervantes, by Plaza de España. Surrounded by a row of olive trees, the three statues are of Cervantes, Don Quixote, and Sancho Panza.

Iglesia de San Marcos (#20; A12), tucked between the two sky-scrapers on C. San Leonardo (M: Pl. España). This little Neoclassical church is composed of five intersecting ellipses; a Euclidean dream, there's not a single straight line in sight.

From Plaza Mayor to the Palacio Real

When Felipe II made Madrid the capital of his empire in 1561, most of the town huddled between the Plaza Mayor and the Palacio Real, stretching north to today's Ópera and south to Plaza Puerta de Moros. Only a handful of medieval buildings remain, but the labyrinthine layout is unmistakable.

Plaza de la Villa (#57; B17, B12), the heart of what was old Madrid (M: Sol). The **Torre de los Lujanes,** a 15th-century building on the east side of the plaza, is the sole remnant of the once lavish Lujanes family residence. The characteristically Habsburg 17th-century **Ayuntamiento** (**Casa de la Villa;** #59; B12, B17) was both the mayor's home and the city jail. As Madrid (and its bureaucracy) grew, officials annexed the neighboring **Casa de Cisneros** (#58; B12, B17), a 16th-century house built in the Plateresque style, named for the work of silversmiths.

Palacio Real (**Palacio de Oriente;** #45; B12), designed partly after Bernini's rejected designs for the Louvre, was built for the first Bourbon King Felipe V to replace the burned Alcázar (M: Ópera). Although only a fragment was completed, it's still one of Europe's most grandiose residences, with 20 square km of tapestry alone. To see the collection of porcelain, tapestries, furniture, armor, and art, stroll on your own or take a guided tour (Spanish, 40min.). The palace's most impressive rooms include the raucously Rococo **Salón de Gasparini** and the **Salón del Trono** (Throne Room). The **Real Oficina de Farmacia** (Royal Pharmacy) features quaint crystal and china receptacles used to cut royal dope. The palace's **Biblioteca** shelves first editions of *Don Quijote* and a Bible in Romany (Gypsy language). The **Real Armería** (Armory) displays El Cid's swords, the armor of Carlos I and Felipe II, and other instruments of medieval warfare and torture. Palace open, except during royal visits, April-Sept. Mon.-Sat. 9am-6:30pm, Sun. 9am-3pm; Oct.-March Mon.-Sat. 9:30am-5pm, Sun. 9am-2pm. 850ptas, students 350ptas. Arrive early to avoid the line.

Plaza de Oriente (#35; B12), across C. Bailén (M: Ópera). The statues of monarchs decorating the square were originally intended for the palace roof, but it was feared that they'd fall off. To the northwest are the **Jardines de Sabatini** (#32; A12), the park of choice for romantics.

Campo del Moro (#44; B11), facing the canal, was opened to the public only 13 years ago. The view of the palace rising on the dark green slope is straight out of a fairy tale.

Catedral de Almudena (#56; B12), Pl. de la Armería (M: Ópera). The controversy surrounding the cathedral's face-lift after a 30 year hibernation becomes obvious upon entering. The psychedelic stained-glass windows clash jarringly with the more conventional altar. Open Mon.-Fri. 10am-1:30pm and 6-8:45pm, Sun. 10am-2pm and 6-8:45pm, closed during mass.

Convento de la Encarnación (#33; A12), just to the north of the Jardines de Sabatini on Pl. Encarnación (M: Pl. España), is the place to go if relics are your style. The convent holds 700 saintly bones. Pedro de Ribera's elegant **Ermita de la Virgen del Puerto** (#55; B11) lies next to the canal, west of the palace.

Parque del Oeste and Ciudad Universitaria

Parque del Oeste (#5; B1) is a large, sloping park noteworthy for its **rosaleda** (rose garden), north of the Palacio Real (M: Argüelles or Moncloa). A yearly competition determines which award-winning rose will be added to the permanent collection.

Templo de Debod (#23; A11; tel. 409 61 65), on Paseo Pinto Rosales, is the only Egyptian temple in Spain. The Egyptian government shipped the 4th-century BC temple stone by stone in appreciation of Spanish archaeologists who helped rescue a series of monuments from advancing waters near the Aswan Dam. Open Tues.-Fri. 10am-2pm and 6-8pm in summer, 10am-2pm and 4-8pm in winter. 300ptas, students 150ptas; free Wed.

Casa de Campo (#9; C1), further down on Paseo Rosales, past the *terrazas* is the *teléferico* (cable car) running between Po. Rosales and the city's largest park. Open Mon.-Thurs. 11am-2:30pm and 4-9pm, Fri. 11am-1:30pm and 4-9pm, Sat.-Sun. 11am-2:30pm and 3:30-10pm; 345ptas one way. From the Casa de Campo end, the amusement park **Parque de Atracciones** (#10; C1) can be found by the sound of roller-coaster-induced screaming (M: Lago or Batán; open Sun.-Fri. noon-11pm, Sat. noon-midnight). The **Zoo** (#49; B16) is five minutes away (open 10am-9:30pm; 1440ptas).

Ermita de San Antonio de la Florida (#5; B1; tel. 542 07 22; M: Príncipe Pío), containing Goya's pantheon, is close to Parque del Oeste at the end of Po. Florida. Goya's frescoed dome arches above his own corpse—but not his skull, which was missing when the remains arrived from France. Open Tues.-Sun. 10am-2pm; free.

Ciudad Universitaria (University City; #11; A5) is quite a distance northwest of the Parque del Oeste and Pl. España (M: Moncloa). A battleground in the Civil War and resistance center during Franco's rule, Spain's largest university educates over 120,000 students per year. The Prime Minister's official residence, the **Palacio de la Moncloa** (#4; B1), can be seen—but not touched—from the road through these grounds.

Cuartel General del Aire (#15; C5), a prime example of Fascist Neoclassicism. The arcaded complex commands the perspective on the other side of Arco de la Victoria. It was to form part of the "Fachada del Manzanares" urban axis linking Moncloa, the Palacio de Oriente and cathedral, and the Iglesia de San Francisco.

El Pardo

El Pardo (#7; C1), built as a hunting lodge for Carlos I in 1547, was subsequently enlarged into the magnificent country palace standing today (15min. from the city center by bus). Franco resided here from 1940-1975, and the palace is still the official reception site for distinguished foreign visitors. Renowned for its collection of tapestries, the palace also holds a little-known Velázquez and Ribera's *Techo de los hombres ilustres* (Ceiling of the Illustrious Men). Open Mon.-Sat. 9:30am-6pm, Sun. 9:30am-2pm. Compulsory 45-min. guided tour in Spanish. 600ptas, students 250ptas, Wed. free for EU citizens. Catch bus #601 from the stop in front of the Ejército del Aire building above M: Moncloa. 15min., 150ptas each way. The palace's **capilla** and the nearby **Casita del Príncipe** (#8; C1), created by Villanueva of El Prado fame, are both free.

ACCOMMODATIONS

The demand for rooms rises dramatically in summer; luckily, Madrid is full of *hostales*. Expect to pay between 1700ptas and 2700ptas per person for a basic *hostal* room, a bit more for a two-star *hostal*, slightly less for a bed in a *pensión*, and even less when visiting during *temporada baja*. Bargaining is always a good idea.

Youth Hostel

Albergue Juvenil Santa Cruz de Marcenado (HI), C. Santa Cruz de Marcenado, 28 (tel. 547 45 32; fax 548 11 96). M: Argüelles. From the Metro, walk 1 block down C. Alberto Aguilera away from C. Princesa, turn right at C. Serrano de Jóven and left on C. Santa Cruz de Marcenado. 75 firm beds in airy rooms fill quickly. HI card required (1800ptas). 3-day max. stay. Reserve a space (by mail or fax only) 15 days in advance, or arrive early and pray. Message board. English spoken. Reception open 9am-10:30pm. Strict curfew 1:30am and lights out at 2am. 950ptas. Over 26 1300ptas. Breakfast included.

Between Puerta del Sol and Palacio Real

This central area is the oldest and one of the most popular in Madrid. Stray several blocks from the Pta. del Sol to find better deals.

Pensión Luz, C. Fuentes, 10, 3rd fl. (tel. 542 07 59), off C. Arenal. M: Sol. Twelve sunny, inviting rooms in an elegant old building. The bathrooms sparkle so much you won't mind sharing. Singles 2000ptas. Doubles 3500ptas, which can convert into triples for 4200ptas. Discounts available for long stays.

Hostal Madrid, C. Esparteros, 6, 2nd fl. (tel. 522 00 60), off C. Mayor. M: Sol. Spacious rooms with wood floors, large windows, TVs, and new bathrooms. Friendly, multilingual proprietors. Singles 3500ptas. Doubles 5000ptas. Triple with balcony 7000ptas.

Hostal Cruz-Sol, Pl. Santa Cruz, 6, 3rd fl. (tel. 532 71 97). Pleasant, ample rooms with cavernous ceilings. No winter heating, but warm and friendly owners. Singles 2000ptas. Doubles 2500ptas. Triples 3000ptas. Showers 200ptas per person, free for singles.

Between Sol and Museo del Prado

This area is just as historic and central, as well as chock full o' bars and restaurants.

Hostal R. Rodriguez, C. Nuñez de Arce, 9, 3rd fl. (tel. 522 44 31). Alluring rooms, including two snazzy triples with classic columns and filmy curtains. Shared baths only. English spoken. Singles 2200ptas. Doubles 3000ptas. Triples 4200ptas.

Hostal Gonzalo, C. Cervantes, 34, 3rd fl. (tel. 429 27 14). M: Antón Martín. Go up C. León 4 blocks and turn right onto C. Cervantes. The friendly proprietors renovated the entire *hostal* without killing its charm. Singles 2200ptas, with bath 3800ptas. Doubles 5000ptas. Triples with bath 6000ptas.

Hostal-Residencia Sud-Americana, Po. del Prado, 12, 6th fl. (tel. 429 25 64), across from the Prado on Pl. Cánovas de Castillo. M: Antón Martín or Atocha. Eight rooms total—all with showers and faux-leather armchairs. Face the Po. de Prado and enjoy a magnificent view, though the summer trees prove an obstacle. Singles 2300ptas. Doubles 4400ptas. One triple 5500ptas.

Calle Fuencarral

Calle Fuencarral is the main traffic pipeline to the Gran Vía. It may be noisier and fumier than the Gran Vía, but it's less expensive and closer to nightlife hubs Malasaña and Chueca.

Hostal Palacios and Hostal Ribadavia, C. Fuencarral, 25, 1st-3rd fl. (tel. 531 10 58 or 531 48 47). M: Gran Vía. Both *hostales* are run by the same cheerful family. **Ribadavia** has pleasant rooms with antique furniture. **Palacios** flaunts brand-spankin' new rooms, all with bath. The soon-to-be-named **1st floor** *hostal* is even brand-spankin' newer. Singles 2300ptas, with bath 2700ptas. Doubles with shower 3700ptas, with bath 4200ptas. Triples with bath 6000ptas. Quad with shower 7000ptas.

Hostal Medieval, C. Fuencarral, 46, 2nd fl. (tel. 522 25 49), on the corner with C. Augusto Figueroa. M: Tribunal. Nothing remotely Dark Age-ish about the lounge, which honors the Spanish royal couple and Real Madrid (the *fútbol* team). The rooms are quirkily decorated with miniature paintings and blossoming plants. Singles with shower 3000ptas. Doubles with shower 4000ptas, with bath 5000ptas. Triples with shower 6000ptas.

Elsewhere

The area behind Gran Vía called **Chueca,** especially along and nea C. Infantas, is about as rich in *hostales* (not to mention restaurant bars, and nightlife) as any of the above districts. It's hip but can b dangerous, especially for solo travelers. Near the train statio Atocha are a handful of *hostales,* the closest down Po. Santa Mari de la Cabeza. Near Chamartín train station budget lodgings are rare

Hotel Monaco, C. Barbieri, 5 (tel. 552 46 30 or 552 46 38; fa 521 16 01). M: Chueca. A former brothel catering to Madrid high society (Alfonso XIII, the king's grandfather, is rumored t have been a frequent visitor). This place proves that kitschy fre coes of Eve-like temptresses, candelabras, and loads of mirrors chic hotel do make. Ask Vogue—they did a spread on Monac Ostentatiously risqué first-floor bedrooms; singles are simpler; a with bath. Treat yourself. Singles 6000ptas. Doubles 8500pta Triples 10,500ptas. Accepts all major credit cards.

Hostal Greco, C. Infantas, 3, 2nd fl. (tel. 522 46 32 or 522 46 3 fax 523 23 61). M: Gran Vía or Chueca. You get lots of bang fo your buck at this art-nouveau *hostal.* Enormous rooms with larg bathrooms, telephones, and personal safes. The owner prefe quiet clientele. Singles (only two—call for a reservatio 3400ptas. Doubles 5300ptas. Triples 7000ptas. Visa, MC.

SEASONAL EVENTS

Festivals

The brochure *Las Fiestas de España,* available at tourist offices ar the bigger hotels, contains historical background and general inf on Spain's festivals.

Madrid's **Carnaval** (the week before Lent), inaugurated in th Middle Ages then prohibited during Franco's dictatorship, exis now as never before. The city bursts with street fiestas, dancin and processions. The Fat Tuesday celebration culminates with th mystifying "Burial of the Sardine."

In late April, the city bubbles with the high-quality **Festiv Internacional de Teatro. Dos de Mayo** (May 2, 1808) comme orates when the people of Madrid rose up against Napolean's inva ing armies; the celebrations center in Malasaña. The May **Fiestas San Isidro,** in honor of Madrid's patron saint, bring concer parades, dancing in the Plaza Mayor, and Spain's best bullfights.

Throughout the summer, the city sponsors the **Veranos de Villa,** an outstanding variety of cultural activities, including free cla sical music concerts, movies in open-air settings, plays, art exhibi an international film festival, opera and *zarzuela* (Spanish operett ballet, and sports. In August, the neighborhoods of **San Cayetan San Lorenzo,** and **La Paloma** have their own festivities in a flu of *madrileñismo.* When the processions, street dancing, traditio games, food, and drink are combined with home-grown hard ro and political slogans, they're a microcosm of contemporary Madr

The **Festivales de Otoño** (Autumn Festivals) from Sept.-No also conjure an impressive array of music, theater, and film. On N 1, **Todos los Santos** (All Saints' Day), an **International Jazz Fe tival** brings great musicians to Madrid.

The **Día de la Constitución** (Day of the Constitution, National Day) on Dec. 6 heralds the arrival of the National Compa of Spanish Classical Ballet in Madrid. Tourist offices in Madrid ha info on all these festivals far in advance. In the weeks preceedi **Navidad** (Christmas), the Plaza Mayor is filled with seasonal sta and displays. **The Noche Vieja** (New Year's Eve) brings thousan of people to the Puerta del Sol for a communal countdown and fi works. For good luck in the coming year, people traditionally co sume one grape for each chime of the clock.

Street Index

23

List of Sights